Don't Settle for the Appetizer!

DR. RENO I. JOHNSON

DON'T SETTLE *for the* APPETIZER!

PURSUE THE
PROMISE
(The Main Course)

FRESH TOUCH PUBLISHING

Fresh Touch Publishing
www.arjm.org
P. O. Box 162392
Altamonte Springs Fl. 32716

Fresh Touch
——PUBLISHING——

© 2019 by DR. RENO I. JOHNSON

All rights reserved solely by the author. The author guarantees all contents are original and do not infringe upon the legal rights of any other person or work. No part of this book may be reproduced in any form without the permission of the author. The views expressed in this book are not necessarily those of the publisher.

Unless otherwise indicated, Scripture quotations taken from the King James Version (KJV)–*public domain.*

Scripture quotations taken from the Holy Bible, New International Version (NIV). Copyright © 1973, 1978, 1984, 2011 by Biblica, Inc.™. Used by permission. All rights reserved.

Printed in the United States of America.

ISBN-13: 978-0-98242-334-9

I DEDICATE THIS BOOK to my eldest daughter Ranae Shakantila Johnson. Love you my big baby! I always knew that there was something special about you. My prayer is that you continue to be determined and persistent as you pursue all that God has in store for you. Never settle for the appetizer, but rather stay hungry and God will deliver to you the main course.

Love always, Daddy!

CONTENTS

Introduction ix

Chapter One: PREPARATION FOR
                         THE PROMISE. 1
Chapter Two: PURSUE THE PROMISE 15
Chapter Three: THE PROMISE WILL MAKE
                         YOU LAUGH 31
Chapter Four: THE PROMISE WILL TAKE
                         YOU HIGHER 47
Chapter Five: AFTERWORD (Remembering
                         the Main Thing) 63

About the Author: 67
Contact the Author: 69
Other Books by the Author: 71

INTRODUCTION

The Promise: More is Coming

I COULDN'T WAIT TO get to the restaurant. It had been a great day with friends at a conference in Atlanta, but I had not eaten much. By evening I had a full, singing heart and an empty, growling stomach.

The prospect of sharing a meal with people I felt close to only heightened my anticipation of what lay ahead. After all, something special can happen when you eat with others. Barriers come down, bridges are built, bonds are formed and strengthened.

Think about some of the rich times in your life, and it's likely that food was involved in some way. From family reunions to business meetings, sitting together and passing plates somehow sweetens the deal or the celebration. Whether they are birthdays, weddings, anniversaries, promotions, retirements, church potlucks, funerals, or tears of joy or sorrow, moments with others can be so much richer when you eat together.

Consider how much food featured in Jesus' ministry. Perhaps it shouldn't be surprising to us; after all, He did call Himself "the bread of life" (John 6:35). While on earth, He fed the crowds of four and five thousand, He lingered over intimate meals with His closest friends, and

He invited Himself to dinner at the house of a social outcast, Zacchaeus the tax collector.

And, of course, at the Last Supper He left His followers with instructions to eat and drink to remember Him in a special way. Their shared table was to be a symbol and sign to the world.

It's interesting to note that when He met two followers on the road to Emmaus, following His resurrection, Luke 24 tells us that though "he expounded unto them in all the scriptures the things concerning himself" (verse 27), it was only later "as he sat at meat with them," (verse 30) — when they were eating together — that their eyes were opened and they realized who He was.

If eating together is good for everyone, how much more so for the people of God. So when we finally took our seats round a table at The Cheesecake Factory, after a long day at Bishop T.D. Jakes' MegaFest gathering, my taste buds were tingling. I asked the waiter to bring us some appetizers while we studied the menu and decided on our main courses. He brought out some Parmesan-and-garlic bread, and southern fried chicken sliders.

They were delicious! I nibbled some and then nibbled some more as I considered the various options on the menu. Having grown up in the Bahamas, close to all that ocean abundance, I knew it had to be seafood, but what kind was difficult to decide. Finally, I asked for fresh-grilled salmon with mashed potatoes and broccoli. I could almost taste it on my tongue.

As we waited for our main courses to arrive, we talked and laughed and shared some more appetizers. Then, at last, my salmon arrived. It looked fresh, firm, and full, beautifully presented — and I could hardly bear the sight of it. You see, I was already full.

I'd eaten so much of what was intended just to whet my appetite for the real feast, that when it came I had no

Introduction

room. In fact, rather than being appealing, it made me feel a bit uncomfortable.

My salmon went back with me to my hotel room that night, where I placed it in the refrigerator. It remained there, completely untouched, for the rest of my stay, eventually being thrown away before I checked out. What a waste.

Perhaps like me, you've gone to a restaurant and ended up taking the main course home with you, uneaten or just partially eaten. Maybe you made the same mistake, filling up on the teaser, what was available there and then, right in front of you, rather than waiting for what you really wanted.

Like me, you settled for less.

Choosing between the good and the best

If we are not careful, we can all too easily repeat my Cheesecake Factory mistake in other areas of our lives, where God has more in mind for us. Instead of waiting for what's best, we settle for what is good.

Instead of waiting for what's best, we settle for what is good.

I think of a young lady I know whose gifted hands won her a job doing nails at a hotel spa. She knew her talents were enough to enable her to start her own business, and she spoke enthusiastically to me about one day doing that.

Several years went by without her making any move to go out on her own, so I finally asked her why. "Well, things are really pretty good the way they are," she told me. "They pay me well, and I have guaranteed work. I am not sure that it's worth the risk."

She too settled, and her desire for more died; the spark dimmed. Sometime later the hotel ended up letting go all the spa staff, and she was forced to revisit and revive her earlier dream.

But there isn't necessarily always a second chance like this. I think of another young lady that I know who was excited to begin studying to be a forensic accountant. She calculated the sort of income she would enjoy once she had qualified and began to daydream about how life would be. But the course work got harder in her second year, and she found the homework overwhelming.

Rather than push through, she decided to look for an easier route. She switched to a business management course whose qualification would secure less pay than the more demanding accounting studies. She settled.

But appetizers are not supposed to work like that. They are intended to stimulate your palate for what's ahead, and to sustain you while you wait, to awaken you for what's coming. Webster's New World College Dictionary also defines appetizer as "a bit of something that excites a desire for more."

How, then, do we end up filling ourselves on what are supposed to be snacks? Sometimes it's because we get distracted and don't realize what we're doing. Sometimes it's because waiting just seems too hard. Sometimes the delays leave us feeling disappointed, so we turn to comfort food; we're tempted to satisfy our appetites prematurely.

Such was the case with Esau. As the older son, he was first in line to inherit on his father, Isaac's death. But Genesis 25 recounts how he gave up his position for a fast-food meal.

Coming in from the fields, tired and hungry, Esau's nostrils caught the aroma of the stew his younger brother, Jacob, was fixing. It smelled good. When Esau asked for a helping, Jacob said he could have one in return for his birthright.

"Behold, I am at the point to die," Esau replied (verse 32). "... what profit shall this birthright do to me?" So he traded what was due him for a quick fix.

Though Esau was in anguish later, when he realized Jacob had tricked him out of his inheritance as the oldest son, what happened was in many ways only a fulfillment of what he himself had set in motion when he settled for less.

You have to stay hungry

It remains true to this day that a quick agreement or settlement, like the one Esau made with Jacob, is not necessarily the best one. Many lawsuits are settled before they get to court because the complainant doesn't want to go through the headache and hassle that may be involved—even though they will likely be awarded more if they hold out.

There are times when the devil will try to persuade you to fill up now on appetizers because he knows what God is getting ready to serve, and he doesn't want you to receive it, or for others to benefit too. Don't fall for it. There is more to come, but you have to be tenacious. You have to stay hungry.

It means being like that old mule that refused to die. The story is told how it fell into a hole that was too deep for it to climb out from, but the animal refused to give up. The owner decided to simply bury the mule in the hole, rather than try to get it out, but every time he would throw a shovel of dirt on

You have to stay hungry.

the mule's back, the animal would shake it off and stamp the dirt down under its feet.

By doing this, the same dirt that had been dumped on it was transformed into another step up right out of the hole. Think about it: the same dirt that has been dumped on you can eventually elevate you if, like that old mule, you get stubborn and refuse to give up.

Don't be like Esau and let your present condition dictate your future. Remember what the apostle Paul said in 2 Corinthians 1:20, "for all the promises of God in him are yea, and in him Amen……" It is up to you to hold on, knowing that he makes "every thing beautiful in his time" (Eccl. 3:11).

It's like being in a race—everything that God has for you is at the finish line; the little that you are experiencing now on your way to the promise is just snacks, appetizers to keep you going until you reach the grand prize.

God does not want the little to satisfy you: little joy, little success, little finances, little favor, little anointing, little power. These are merely appetizers intended to fuel your desire for the main course, your promise. And how much more God has in store for you? According to 1 Corinthians 2:9: "Eye hath not seen, nor ear heard, neither have entered into the heart of man, the things which God hath prepared for them that love him."

There is more coming

Wherever you are in life right now, God has more for you. In 2 Corinthians 3:18 we read that we are all being changed "into the same image from glory to glory," as we become more like Jesus. There is more ahead for you: the anointing that you are flowing in now is a taster, the relationships you are enjoying, the financial status you are experiencing, are all just snacks. Don't become full and settle here. Leave room.

Introduction

The enemy will send people into your life to distract, detour, discourage, dishearten, and disconcert you. If anyone ever experienced that, and if ever anyone had reason to settle, it was the apostle Paul. Yet he was determined to go the extra mile, to be sure to get all that God had for him and to do all that God had for him to do.

While he was in Caesarea, on his third missionary journey, Paul was prophesied to by Agabus. Acts 21:11 tells how "... he took Paul's girdle, and bound his own hands and feet, and said, Thus saith the Holy Ghost, so shall the Jews at Jerusalem bind the man that owneth this girdle, and shall deliver him into the hands of the Gentiles."

With such a warning, Paul might have been forgiven for thinking, *Okay, I have done enough. I'm not going any further.* Indeed, others encouraged him that way: "And when we heard these things, both we, and they of that place, besought him not to go up to Jerusalem" (Acts 21:12).

But despite having experienced God's power operating and flowing through him in signs, wonders, and miracles, Paul knew there was yet something more, a greater dimension in God he had not yet known, and he wanted to discover it. Paul's palate was stimulated because of what he had already experienced.

And so he responded, "... what mean ye to weep and to break mine heart? For I am ready not to be bound only, but also to die at Jerusalem for the name of the Lord Jesus" (Acts 21:13). In effect, he was saying, *Friends, I am going all the way; not the appetizer only, but the full course!*

God's call on your life may not be taking you to Rome, like Paul. But He does have a destiny in mind for you, something He calculated from the foundation of the world, when He set aside favor allotted to you. What you have experienced thus far is the foretaste. Increase and elevation is the portion coming for those prepared to endure and to wait.

I think of my dear sister, Lahoma. With six children of her own, she yet somehow found the capacity to care for our younger siblings, when our mother died. Times were hard and demanding, but she was determined to pursue a career in nursing.

She began her studies despite being incredibly busy and facing discouragement and even opposition from some teachers, friends, and even family. There were times when she would call me in tears, saying that it was all too hard, the obstacles were too great, but that she couldn't and wouldn't settle.

She kept at it, first becoming a Certified Nursing Assistant, then a Registered Medical Assistant. From there she advanced to become a Licensed Practical Nurse, and then a Registered Nurse. And still she is not finished, currently pursuing a Bachelor of Science degree in nursing.

Her life has been challenging, but it has also been transformed because she refused to settle for appetizers. She is going after the main course, and I am so proud of her example.

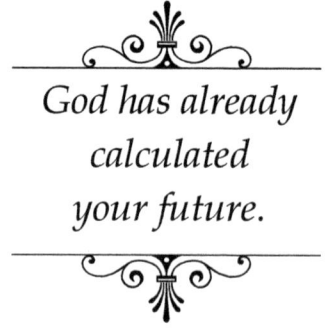

God has already calculated your future.

I believe that there is more ahead for you, too. You are about to walk through double doors of opportunity and prosperity, so get ready to enjoy the main course — the anointing, the favor, the overflow. Prepare to move to another level because God has already calculated your future. Don't settle for the appetizer!

What does that mean for you? In the following pages we are going to look at some of the reasons we can settle for less, some of the ways the enemy attempts to keep God's people from enjoying all that He wants to serve, how to keep sight of what really matters, and how to endure.

Introduction

We'll mine lessons from the lives of three famous figures from the Bible: Jacob, Abraham, Caleb. Though their stories are very different, in each, food appropriately features prominently in some way, and encourages us: Don't settle for the appetizer!

Chapter One

PREPARATION FOR THE PROMISE

IF THIS BOOK were an advertisement for a new wonder drug, then this would be where the asterisk would go. You know, you open a magazine and there's a photo of someone looking happy and healthy, with promises of FULLER LIFE or MAXIMUM VITALITY, or something like that.

Only, the words in big type have that little star symbol next to them, and when you look down at the foot of the page, there are lines and lines of small-print text warning you about all the things that could possibly go wrong if you do take this new medication. Television and radio adverts do a similar thing, only the announcer gabbles through the list as quickly as possible at the end, so you can't really understand what they are saying.

There's one big difference between this book and those adverts, however. The ads are talking about possible consequences, how a good thing could turn into something bad. What I want to talk about is the other way round. I mean requirements, the potentially difficult things that you need to know about that will *lead* to your good thing, if you let them, not possibly *result* from it.

This is your preparation for the promise. Later on, I'm going to be sharing some advice for how to be sure that you receive what God has in store for you, but first you need to recognize that some waiting is inevitable.

It's probably not because your promise isn't ready — remember that Jesus produced vintage wine in an instant, at the wedding in Cana. It's that *you* are not ready for *it*. God has to work with and in you to bring you to the place where you are ready — and that's probably going to mean some dry and dusty times.

You wouldn't buy a car or a computer that hadn't been tested, right? You'd want to know that it could function effectively. When I ran a wave runner rental company in my businessman days, I checked out every new machine before it went into service. I had to be sure they would deliver the goods.

Companies don't hire new employees without being sure that they are capable of the tasks they will be given. Depending on the level of responsibility, the job testing can be very demanding. A young woman I know spent several weeks doing preliminary training with a new company before sitting a test that required a ninety percent pass minimum. She fell just two percentage points short, but they still let her go.

As far as they were concerned, she was not ready.

God wants to know that you are ready. The Greek word used for "preparation" in the New Testament is *hetomazia*, which means to be ready, fitness, preparedness. In other words, what God is about to do for you, you have got to be fit, spiritually, to handle. He has to process you before He can bless you. And that is not likely to happen overnight.

When the children of Israel were led out of slavery in Egypt, they were on their way to the land flowing with milk and honey that God had promised them (Exod. 3:8). But they would spend forty years in the wilderness.

Part of that extended detour was a consequence of their disbelief and doubt, when the spies who had gone to check out the homeland God had said was theirs came back warning that it was occupied by giants, and impossible to possess. The people chose to believe ten fearful spies over two faithful ones (Num. 13:31). As a result, God swore that no one from that generation would set foot in the Promised Land except for the two resolute spies, Joshua and Caleb.

But there was another factor. When the Israelites were finally poised to enter the land, Deuteronomy 8:2-3 records Moses telling them:

> And thou shalt remember all the way which the Lord thy God led thee these forty years in the wilderness, to humble thee, and to prove thee, to know what was in thine heart, whether thou wouldest keep his commandments, or no. And he humbled thee, and suffered thee to hunger, and fed thee with manna, which thou knewest not, neither did thy fathers know; that he might make thee know that man doth not live by bread only, but by every word that proceedeth out of the mouth of the Lord doth man live.

Later, he reminded them that God "fed thee in the wilderness with manna, which thy fathers knew not, that he might humble thee, and that he might prove thee, to do thee good at thy latter end" (Deut. 8:16).

God wanted the Israelites to learn some things before they entered into His promise. There are things for us to learn, too, as we follow in their footsteps.

Life in the wilderness

One thing is for sure, John the Baptist was something of an exception: most people wouldn't choose to go and live in the wilderness. It's inhospitable, it's inconvenience, it's insufficiency. Too much nothing and not enough more.

The landscape is bleak: it can go from searing heat in the day to shivery cold at night. It is dry and barren. There's little sustenance to be found, while dangers abound from roaming wild beasts and deadly small insects. There are wolves and hyenas, snakes and scorpions.

Then there is the lack of clear direction, just endless horizons wherever you look. No sense of where you should head, no feeling of purpose, just day after boring day of the same. And maybe you're enduring this alone or — possibly even worse — with others who are driving you crazy. It's a place of all kinds of opposition.

Now, this kind of wilderness isn't only to be experienced beyond the city limits, out in remote geographical places. It could be in a home where relationship temperatures soar and drop, or at a workplace where others are looking to devour you. God will even use the cat and the dog in your yard to test you before He blesses you. Your wilderness could even be in church!

The natural reaction when we find ourselves in a situation like this is to look for the quickest way out. That's only human. But God takes us there for a reason, so we need to be sure to cooperate. Don't wriggle!

One desert may look pretty much like another — lots of sand and not much else. But your wilderness has been crafted for you individually by God! It is idiosyncratic, tailor-made for you. God will give you just the right person to get on your nerves. He will set you on just the right job where they are going to try to take you down. This is all not to crush you, but to cultivate you.

Take confidence in the fact that you don't end up in the wilderness by accident but by God's plan. And having taken you in, He will lead you out in due time. As David wrote in Psalm 37:23, "The steps of a good man are ordered by the LORD: and he delighteth in his way."

Lessons in the wilderness

When God takes us into the wilderness, it's often to develop four things in us.

1. Capacity.

Like my old wave runners, God wants to know that we won't sink! Too many Christians start out on fire, but then flame out. They get a taste of the good things God has for them, and they forget the source of them. They start to think that they may have had something to do with it all.

This can lead people one of two ways. Some sadly forget that God is the source of their new blessing. They buy that new car with the extra money they are making, but instead of driving it to church to celebrate, they go the other way, heading to the club to party.

Or they begin to believe their own publicity, and start to think that, you know what, they really are all that. They start looking down on other people instead of keeping looking up at God.

Either way, it's clear that they are not ready for more. God wants to know whether He can trust you with what He has in store.

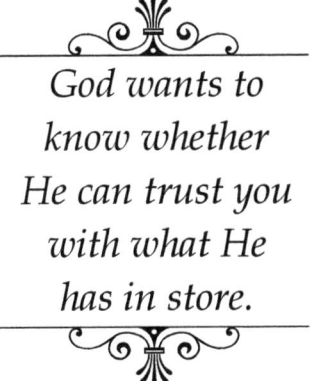

God wants to know whether He can trust you with what He has in store.

2. Quality.

Testing proves what we are really made of. Difficulties are like a pressure washer, revealing our true colors underneath. What do you say when you stub your toe in the dark, or when someone gets on your last half of a nerve? That sharp word that pops out of your mouth when things are going all wrong isn't really "not like me," it's actually the true you that is exposed when the nice exterior we usually manage to keep up gets torn down.

Remember that Jesus said, "But those things which proceed out of the mouth come forth from the heart; and they defile the man" (Matt. 15:18). Most of us find it easier to see others' weaknesses than our own. We often don't see our weaknesses until circumstances reveal them.

The Bible has several references to how God refines us in the same way that metalworkers would purify silver and gold—heating it up so that the dirt and dross would rise to the surface so that it could be scooped away. The Greek word used in the New Testament, *docomazo*, means to test, to prove, or to approve. In Psalm 66, the writer recalls how God led His people out of Egypt, parting the Red Sea, before adding, "For you, God, tested us; you refined us like silver." (verse 10, NIV).

God wants to know our hearts are set on Him whatever our circumstances. It's one thing to praise Him when everything is going right, when you have plenty of money in the bank and a sweet honey at home. But what about when the money is tight and she or he wants to fight? Can you still declare that God is good, all the time?

Your time in the wilderness will bring to the surface things God wants to remove from your life. Don't shy away from this—He's not exposing these parts of you to shame you but to bring you into the light and free you from them. Cooperate with Him.

God is more interested in our character, our moral fiber, than he is in our comfort. If you feel God turning up the heat, welcome it. The hotter the fire, the more it burns out all those things that can hinder us from the great things that God has in store for us.

3. Humility.

Even people who don't read the Bible can quote at least one verse, though they may not be aware of it — Proverbs 16:18, which warns that "pride goeth before destruction." Or as we'd say today, Pride goes before a fall. Maybe that's because proud people have their noses in the air, so they can't see clearly where they are going, and end up tripping.

Arrogant people are no fun to be around. Those kind of folks who feel like if they don't get to do it just their way, then it can't be done, that they are the cream in your coffee and the sugar in your tea, are often like the seed sown on stony ground in Jesus's parable. They spring up fast, but they soon wilt away. I can think of one gifted minister who rose to prominence, but in short time found people deserting his church because of his high and mighty manner.

Do you treat people well however they treat you? What about when they say bad things about you? Do you choose to still love them? Would you be able to tell them that you are still on their side? Would you give them some money for food if you knew they were hungry?

Or it may be that God will put you in a position where you need to go and ask others for help. For some, that's a really hard pill to swallow, because they don't want to appear weak and incapable. But it might be that you need to learn that God wants His people to be interdependent, to be His body with its different parts working together. God sometimes causes us to be in a place of dependency so that He can break us from our haughtiness and our arrogance. We can choose to humble ourselves before God, or He will do the job for us by bringing about circumstances beyond our control!

4. Dependency.

Milk and honey don't just arrive at your table. They have to be gathered and harvested. You have to care for the cows and milk them, tend to the beehives and gather the honey. After a time, it's possible to forget that you're still only working with natural resources that come from God, and maybe start to credit yourself for the good things that are on the table.

Before they got to feast on milk and honey, the Israelites spent years eating what came directly from the hand of God—His daily ration of manna and quail. They *knew* they were dependent on God's provision. He was literally their source of life.

Moses reminded the people, "He humbled you, causing you to hunger and then feeding you with manna, which neither you nor your ancestors had known, to teach you that man does not live on bread alone but on every word that comes from the mouth of the LORD" (Deut. 8:3, NIV).

When the devil tempted Jesus after His own time in the wilderness, he tried to appeal to Jesus's weakened flesh, suggesting He turn stones into bread. Jesus's answer? He went back to the Israelites' time in the wilderness, declaring, "It is written, Man shall not live by bread alone, but by every word that proceedeth out of the mouth of God" (Matt. 4:4).

The wilderness reveals to us that it was not our strength that made us prosper. I don't care what you have today: you did not get it on your own. It is the hand of God. The wilderness is to show us that we cannot do it without God. When we are in that dry, barren land, when there is nobody to call, when no one is lending a helping hand, the only thing we can do is lift up our eyes unto the hills, to God, from where our help comes (Ps. 121:1).

The wilderness is also a time when you need to bring your natural desires and appetites under control. It is to teach you that you need more than a loaf of bread, you need the Bread of Life Himself.

Protection and preparation

The wilderness is not only for us, it is for others too. Time with God in the wilderness prepares you for the good things that He has for you — and better positions you to be a source of good things for others.

If you're not strong enough to lift what God wants to give you, it's going to cause pain. You are going to throw your back out trying to lift that thing. We've all read stories of people who have suddenly come into a lot of money, only to end up with all sorts of problems — divorce, drugs, depression. Many have said they wished they had never gotten all that money. They weren't ready for it.

In that sense, the wilderness is God's protection, keeping you from disaster. Think of how the young man in the parable of the prodigal son got what was coming to him before the proper time. The money was really the inheritance he was not due to receive until his father's death, but he asked for it while the older man was still alive. And he ended up in a pig sty.

Some people get more than they can handle directly as a result of their greed, like the prodigal son, while others manipulate or use other people's power and position. Whatever the route, it will become a dead end.

Testing in the wilderness will strengthen your faith so that you can handle what God wants to give you. But in addition to bringing about God's blessing in your life, it can bring God's blessing to others' lives. That shouldn't be surprising, because when God first made His promise to Abraham, He told him, "And I will make of thee a great nation, and I will bless thee, and make thy name great; and thou shalt be a blessing" (Gen. 12:2).

Testing creates a platform from which we can minister to others. After all, you cannot really tell anybody else that God will supply their needs if He has never done it for you. You cannot tell someone else that God is a healer if you have never been sick and God had to touch your body. You cannot tell someone else that God will make a way out of no way when you have always had things going the way you want them to go.

But when you have come through the darkness, you can tell someone else with conviction that, as Psalm 27:1 declares, "The LORD is my light and my salvation; whom shall I fear? the LORD is the strength of my life; of whom shall I be afraid?" You can echo David's further words, "Though an host should encamp against me, my heart shall not fear: though war should rise against me, in this will I be confident" (verse 3).

We are blessed to be a blessing. 2 Corinthians 1:4 says that God "comforteth us in all our tribulation, that we may be able to comfort them which are in any trouble, by the comfort wherewith we ourselves are comforted of God."

Testing is inevitable

When you find yourself being led into the wilderness, don't despair—you are in good company. Think of all the great characters in the Bible who went through terribly difficult times before they came into all that God had promised them. Moses, Abraham, Joseph, David, Paul, and others. They suffered rejection, loneliness, false accusations and imprisonment as they walked through their proving ground. Even Jesus, perfect as He was, had His time in the wilderness before He stepped into His ministry.

In fact, I am aware of only two men in the Bible who were called to great things who did not seem to go through any kind of real wilderness experience, and in each case it did not end well.

Saul, the man chosen as the first king of Israel, was later consumed by jealousy. He couldn't stand the thought that the people loved and admired his young general, David, more than him. His insecurity ate him up. In due course, when Solomon took over the throne from his father, David, he was consumed by his own passions. His unchecked appetites devoured him.

Neither man seemed to have benefited from having their inner lives strengthened and refined through time in the wilderness. As a consequence, their "bowls" were not strong enough to hold the blessing God wanted to pour into their lives. They cracked under the pressure of His goodness, as it were.

With all that in mind, let me encourage you to always keep in mind that, even if you are not going through a wilderness time right now, others around you might be. Sometimes we can see someone having difficulties and become a bit judgmental, even if we don't say anything out loud. We can assume their challenges must be a result of something they have done wrong, or not done. But it could just be they are in their wilderness, as God prepares them for His promise.

Don't be too quick to judge. After all, a judge or jury delivers their verdict only after hearing all the evidence. You may not know all there is to know about a situation. What seems to be God's rebuke could be His refining. What appears to be a season of setback could actually be their time of revelation and elevation. Those folks going through a hard time might just need a word of encouragement from you.

Finally, don't worry what others think about you while you are in the wilderness. Their opinion does not count; you just want to know that God is pleased with you. As you surrender to His process, you come to the place where He can bless.

I'm not saying that God's blessings can be earned, but there is a link between obedience and blessing. Isaiah 1:19 says, "If ye be willing and obedient, ye shall eat the good of the land..." God's blessings cannot be bought, but in another way they will cost you. Are you prepared to pay the price to receive what God wants to give you?

If the answer is yes, then be expectant. Many times God will send someone with a word of encouragement, assuring you that blessing is coming but forewarning you of a test before the best. That has happened for me several times, giving me confidence to persevere when things got hard.

God told Abram that His descendants would one day be as countless as the stars in the sky. However, He went on, "Know of a surety that thy seed shall be a stranger in a land that is not theirs, and shall serve them; and they shall afflict them four hundred years" (Gen. 15:13). There would be hard times ahead, but don't you dare settle for the appetizer!

Don't be like some who, when faced with the wilderness, get distracted. They take their eyes off God and turn them on lesser things. They turn to other people or possessions for comfort or validation. Others can get too focused — on the wrong thing. They misinterpret what is happening as something keeping them from what God

There would be hard times ahead, but don't you dare settle for the appetizer!

intends, so they just double-down on trying to overcome whatever hurdle is in front of them.

I did that for a while when I first knew God was calling me to change my life's direction. I was excited at the prospect of serving Him in ministry, but I tried to hold onto my businesses even as they started to decline. I just kept investing more effort and money in keeping them going, to no return. Finally I realized that I was working against God rather than with Him, and that He was using the circumstances I faced to help redirect and reposition me.

Whatever you find yourself facing in the wilderness, remember that difficult as it may seem, it is not intended to prevent you from receiving God's blessing, it is to prepare you to. Build up the spiritual muscle you will need to carry what God is bringing. Choose to become better, not bitter.

You are being prepared for the promise. Don't settle for the appetizer!

Chapter Two

PURSUE THE PROMISE

GOD HAS A feast in store for you; that's the good news. I hope that you are rubbing your hands and licking your lips in anticipation of all that He wants to do in your life. He desires to bless you richly, but not just so that you can sit back and enjoy it all yourself. He wants to bless you so that you may in turn be a channel of his blessings to others.

That's always been His intent, ever since He told Abram to pack up and set out for a new land. So you should be expectant of God's blessings. But there's something else you need to know: those blessings probably aren't going to come to you on a silver platter. Sometimes they come in a rush, that's true, but more often than not it's more like the Gold Rush — you have to go after them.

While you can't hurry God's timing, or force His hand, it's no good just sitting around twiddling your thumbs, waiting for Him to bring you all that He has in mind. You are going to have to pursue God's promise for you.

It's a pattern we see repeated time and again in the Bible. Abram was told his descendants would be as numerous as the stars in the sky (Gen. 15:5), but he had to leave home for parts unknown, and trust God even when it seemed impossible he and Sarai would ever have children.

When the Israelites finally entered the Promised Land after their forty-year detour in the wilderness, they didn't have instant access to all the milk and honey they had been told was there. They would have to take possession of the land bit by bit, fighting to take hold of what was rightfully theirs.

Joseph had been told he would rise to a position of authority, and might have been forgiven for thinking he had made it when he was placed in charge of the house of Potiphar, one of the most powerful people in Egypt. But God had in mind an even more lofty place, at Pharaoh's palace—though getting there would involve Joseph going to prison en route.

David won national acclaim as Saul's champion, the people's favorite, but his destiny was to be king of Israel—even though the road to the throne would take him via a cave. Don't settle for the appetizer!

The apostle Paul acknowledged in his letter to the Philippians that achieving the "high calling" of God was not an instant thing for him. Rather, he wrote how "this one thing I do, forgetting those things which are behind, and reaching forth unto those things which are before, I press toward the mark..." (3:13-14).

We have to pursue the promise.

I'm in that process myself. I thought I'd made it as a young man, with multiple businesses and more than thirty employees. I was enjoying some of the rewards that come with financial success. But then it all came crashing down overnight, and I was left with nothing.

God got my attention through these circumstances, and turned my heart to serving in His kingdom rather than building my own empire. As I did, He began to speak to me about the future, in my spirit and through other godly men and women who told me they saw

God's hand on my life. His message: I would achieve more going about the business of the kingdom than I ever had or could have in the business world, if only I would go all-out for Him.

So I began serving in my local church, assisting the pastor in any way he needed. No task was too small. Then came an opportunity to serve in the media department, helping to run the cameras, and later an invitation to lead the men's group. In due course I was asked to lead praise and worship, and given the opportunity to preach and was finally ordained as a minister.

In time, I felt God's direction to step out on my own, founding a new church. I began to receive invitations to minister elsewhere, and have begun to travel internationally to preach. I have written several books. It has all been good, but I know there is yet more ahead, and I do not intend to settle for the appetizer. I want all that God has got for me.

If we can see the design of God's wish to bless us in the life of Abram, who would become Abraham, then we can learn a lot about pursuing the promise of those blessings from the life of his grandson, Jacob.

The younger twin born to Isaac, Abraham's son, Jacob knew a thing or two about the power of appetites, of course. Remember how he took advantage of his older brother Esau's unchecked hunger, when Esau came in from the fields:

> And Esau said to Jacob, Feed me, I pray thee, with that same red pottage; for I am faint: therefore was his name called Edom. And Jacob said, Sell me this day thy birthright. And Esau said, Behold, I am at the point to die: and what profit shall this birthright do to me? And Jacob said, Swear to me this day; and he sware unto him: and he sold

> his birthright unto Jacob. Then Jacob gave Esau bread and pottage of lentiles; and he did eat and drink, and rose up, and went his way: thus Esau despised his birthright.
> – Genesis 25:30-34

And later, Jacob would use his father, Isaac's hunger as a way to appropriate the blessing due to his brother. Genesis 27 recounts how when Isaac asked for a last favorite steak as he lay on his death bed, Jacob conspired with his mother, Rebekah, to pass himself off as Esau and secure their father's blessing.

This reversal of the siblings' order had been spoken of ahead of time, when Rebekah prayed during her pregnancy. Genesis 25:23 records, "And the Lord said unto her, Two nations are in thy womb, and two manner of people shall be separated from thy bowels; and the one people shall be stronger than the other people; and the elder shall serve the younger."

In the events that unfolded subsequently, as Jacob pursued the blessing that he had been given, are some lessons and encouragement for us as we follow after ours.

Reject the status quo

Grieved as he was by Jacob's subterfuge, Isaac appears to have resigned himself to the new order in his family.

In Genesis 28:1-2 we read, "And Isaac called Jacob, and blessed him, and charged him, and said unto him, Thou shalt not take a wife of the daughters of Canaan. Arise, go to Padanaram, to the house of Bethuel thy mother's father; and take thee a wife from thence of the daughters of Laban thy mother's brother."

In the days before highways and airplanes it would have been much easier for Jacob to look for a wife from closer to home, but the woman he needed to meet to be part of God's future for him was not there. In other words, he could not settle for the easy, stay-at-home route.

In the same way, your blessing may not be conveniently at hand. Don't limit what you think God can do by what you see around you. Be open and expectant.

Be open and expectant.

Obedience is essential

He probably had questions, but Jacob did as he was directed, setting out for Padanaram. Doing what's right is always important, even when we don't see the rhyme or the reason. But the decisions you make today are critical in determining the outcome of your life, because they will put you in the place God has in mind—figuratively and literally, as with Jacob—to fulfill all His purposes.

Your choices today will determine where you will be in another year—your position in the kingdom, in business, at work, in your relationships, in your finances, and so forth. While you may not be clear about what God has for you next year, there are things you can be sure He wants of you of today: to love Him, love His people, and love those who do not yet know Him!

Many Christians get hung up about "guidance" on things like where they should live, what they should do for a job, and who they should marry. These are important questions, certainly, but as we wait on those answers God has made it clear what He wants us to do in the everyday:

"He hath shewed thee, O man, what is good; and what doth the Lord require of thee, but to do justly, and to love mercy, and to walk humbly with thy God?" (Micah 6:8).

Jacob's obedience was critical in his receiving all that the blessing entailed. If he had looked for a wife among the Canaanites, he would never have experienced all that he did.

Take God seriously

We need to value what is important to God. Remember how Esau carelessly gave up his God-given birthright because he was hungry, swapping a rich inheritance for a few cheap mouthfuls.

Don't be like Esau: don't settle for the appetizer!

It's sobering to consider that when we treat lightly the things God wants to give us, we offend Him. In Malachi 1:2-3 He says, "... I have loved Jacob, but Esau I have hated, and I have turned his hill country into a wasteland and left his inheritance to the desert jackals" (NIV).

When we reject God's desire to drive us forward, to bless us, we don't just go into neutral; we can find ourselves in reverse. There's God's way or there's the opposite. Remember when Moses gathered the people before they were to enter the Promised Land and told them, "This day I call the heavens and the earth as witnesses against you that I have set before you life and death, blessings and curses. Now choose life..." (Deut. 30:19, NIV).

That is a serious choice. But the good news is that it doesn't have to be a hard one to make. Moses had assured the people:

> For this commandment which I command thee this day, it is not hidden from thee, neither is it far off. It is not in heaven, that thou shouldest say, Who shall go up for us to heaven, and bring it unto us, that we may hear it, and do it? Neither is it beyond the

sea, that thou shouldest say, Who shall go over the sea for us, and bring it unto us, that we may hear it, and do it? But the word is very nigh unto thee, in thy mouth, and in thy heart, that thou mayest do it.
- Deuteronomy 30:11-14

Be ready to move

Jacob moved towards his destiny, even though it probably did not make much sense to him. He was in familiar territory, where he likely knew all the women in that region. Yet here he was being told to leave everything he knew and go somewhere else.

He was willing to pursue the promise!

Pursuing your promise may take you out of your comfort zone.

Pursuing your promise may take you out of your comfort zone too, away from what and who you know. That then puts you in a situation where you have to rely more on God. As the old saying goes, "When God stretches you, it is so that he can occupy a bigger space."

Sometimes we need to move not because we are relying on what we know but who we know, because we're eating at someone else's table, as it were, when God has a setting of our own in mind. I wonder if Jacob's friends questioned his decision to move away, inviting him to stay and eat with them? His attitude was, *Thanks for the invitation, but I don't want to eat from your table. There is a table that is spread with my name on it, and I am going to find it.*

Be alert for the unexpected

When Jacob reached a well in "the land of the people of the east" (Gen.29:1), he didn't seem to know where he was; he asked the shepherds he met there where they came from. He certainly was not aware that he had arrived at the doorway to his destiny. Wow!

If you're feeling a bit lost right now, take some encouragement from Jacob's experience. You are not alone. And, like him, you could be very close to your blessing. Don't settle for the appetizer!

As has been said, it is darkest before the dawn. Jacob's example reminds us that the greatest things that God has in store for us often appear seemingly out of nowhere. In other words, if you can see it, then that isn't it. If you are around it every day and it's casual to you, that's not it.

Though Jacob had been given a general direction in which to head, he needed help along the way—the shepherds were able to tell him that he had reached his goal. Though they didn't know it themselves, the shepherds were in the exact right place: and sometimes we may need assistance along the way from people unaware that they are a crucial part of our reaching where we need to go. We should be open to seeing and hearing God in what may seem to be very ordinary, everyday encounters. Be alert for the unexpected!

Clear some people out

When Jacob learned that he had arrived at Laban's place and the shepherds pointed out that Rachel was on her way to the well, he tried to scooch them away by telling them to go water the sheep. It seemed that he didn't want any distractions or interruptions as he met Rachel.

Similarly, you may have to clear some people out of your life before God sends what he's got for you. Maybe they are a bad influence: 1 Corinthians 15:33 declares, "Be not deceived: evil communications corrupt good manners." Or perhaps they are just a distraction, or discouraging you from pursuing God. Relationships greatly shape and influence our lives, for good or otherwise.

It's not just people that may need to go, either; are there sins, attitudes, areas of unforgiveness that need to be dealt with, cleared away? You may have to make some decisions before God sends what He has promised you.

Listen to your heart

Don't be surprised if there are tears as you draw closer to the promise, just as Jacob wept when he met Rachel (Gen. 29:11). Some people may think you're crying because you're sad, but you know it's because you're glad. These are not tears of sorrow, but tears of joy.

I'm not suggesting that you rely just on your feelings to guide you, but there is a deep joy that goes beyond mere feelings, something down in our spirit, that witnesses, "This is God."

I believe that was what moved Jacob that he wept from a sense of the goodness of his heavenly father. He had obeyed God in journeying to a strange land, and though he had not known where he was, God had led him to the very place and people he needed to find. This was not a coincidence, this was providence. Don't settle for the appetizer, wait for the main course!

Neither will your promise come about through mere happenstance, but through providence — the certainty that God is constantly in control of everything, at all times. Even when we are in the dark. No wonder Jacob wept as he recognized the favor God had bestowed upon him!

Be on your guard

Satan doesn't give up easily. He wants to do everything in his power to keep us from what God has for us. If he can't dissuade or discourage us from setting out on the journey, and if he can't divert or detour us along the way, he will try to dupe us just before we receive what is coming.

We need to be on our guard when we sense we're arriving at our destination. When we are so close to the end, that's when we can begin to coast, if we are not careful. The enemy is waiting for an opportunity to pounce and keep us from all that God intends. There will often be a trick from Satan before the treat from God.

A good friend of mine, Glenville Davis, started out as a bank teller, with an associate's degree. After earning his bachelor's degree in business management, he was promoted to supervisor. But he didn't stop there; he went on to get his master's degree in business administration and was appointed customer service manager.

Glenville could have been tempted to rest on his laurels at this point, but during his studies he had developed a passion for teaching. So he studied for a doctorate in business administration, becoming a highly respected lecturer at one of the top universities in the Bahamas. He kept his eyes on the prize.

Glenville didn't settle for the appetizer, but pursued the main course!

The enemy wants you to settle for just the engagement, rather than marriage, for a high school diploma, rather than pursue a college degree, for an associate degree, rather than a masters or doctorate, to be a nurse, rather than a doctor, to be a paralegal, rather than become a lawyer, to be a regular Christian, rather than becoming a World changer. He wants you to stay in the minor league; he just wants you to settle. Don't settle for the appetizer!

Letting his guard down, Jacob ended up with Leah instead of his true love, her sister Rachel; this was all the doings of Laban their father (Gen 29:15-28). It's not completely clear what the Bible means when it says that Leah had "weak eyes" (Gen. 29:17, NIV), though the eyes were a main feature of beauty in the ancient world. The suggestion is that Leah may have been plain, without appeal, because the same verse goes on "but Rachel had a lovely figure and was beautiful."

Counterfeits can be hard to spot. Sometimes they actually have some of the same things that are in the real deal. Heresy always mixes in an element of truth; that's how people get lured into it. Leah shared some of the same DNA as Rachel. But she was not the true prize Jacob had been waiting for. She was not the main course.

Pursue the promise!

Watch out for lookalikes

It may seem hard to believe Jacob could be foolish enough to end up with the wrong person, but let's try to give him the benefit of the doubt. The lights are low, you're finally with the one you've yearned for all these years; are you really going to suspect it's someone else? Are you going to say, *Hey, let me just check,* and switch the lights on?

It's not that hard to fall for a lookalike. You may have experienced something like it before. You are at a place where God has said He is going to open something up and, suddenly, there are three doors right in front of you! Which way to go?

Or maybe it's a door that takes you back the way you have just come. This happened to me after I lost everything I had and began to pursue God. Some good friends who knew of my past successes came and made me an offer for me to join them in a new business venture. On the face of it, it seemed like a great opportunity. But I had to decline their kind invitation, as I knew it would be taking me in the wrong direction.

Be cautious. Is this sudden career opportunity your destiny or might it be a diversion to keep you from the real thing? You've waited a long time for the right person to come into your life and then this man or woman suddenly appears out of nowhere. Be careful; they could be your soul mate, or they could be a seducer sent to keep you from the real one who's coming along soon.

It's so important not to rush into big decisions without seeking God's clarity and confirmation. Too many Christians, it seems to me, jump into things—relationships, work opportunities, even ministry—without really being sure that they are His will, because they seem so appealing, and then just expect Him to bless them anyway.

You can't go and make your own choice and decisions and then say, *God, I need you now to rest your hands on this.* If you go to the car lot and buy a vehicle because it looks nice but don't check under the hood, don't be surprised if it comes to a smoking halt halfway down the street, as you cry, *God, why did you let this happen to me?* He is wondering why you didn't check in with Him first; He would have told you it was a lookalike.

Yes, He is a forgiving God when we admit our mistakes, and He can work even our wrong choices to the good when we confess where we have erred. But there's a difference between God redeeming things and blessing what He has planned and purposed. There are consequences to our decisions and actions. If I spend my money foolishly and then repent, I can expect God to help me turn things around in due course, but I may have to go through some rough days because of my stupidity. Watch out for lookalikes!

Sober up

Buyer's remorse. The cold light of morning. Call it what you will, you have probably experienced a situation where you did or bought something that seemed to fulfill all your dreams, only for that full, sweet moment to give way to a horrible sense of emptiness.

That was Jacob's experience when he woke the day after his wedding night to discover that the woman sharing his bed was not Rachel but Leah. Maybe Laban had been generous when he poured the wine for the wedding toasts, or perhaps the low lights had been enough to keep Jacob from realizing there had been a switch. Whatever happened, Jacob's heart sank.

Can you identify? You thought that small paycheck you received was great. You were satisfied with that beat-up old car. You were content in your fixer-up home. They were enough for the moment.

But now, you realize that you have settled for less. Maybe you figured, hey, your family has to eat, and you've got mortgage, and so you rationalized that you couldn't walk away from the job offer in front of you.

But now it's morning, and you have come to your senses. In the half-light things seemed fine, but not now in the bright dawn. *What am I doing here?* you ask yourself. Don't settle for the appetizer!

Pursue the promise!

Remember the well

If Jacob's morning-after predicament is yours right now, let me encourage you. It's not over! Yes, you got full with the appetizer, but God still has the main course He has been preparing for you. All is not lost.

God will yet bring you what He has ordained for you. It may just require a further season of sacrifice. Are you willing to go further to secure what God has promised?

Jacob could have decided that he would make do with Leah, but no. He fulfilled his obligations toward Leah, but his heart was still for Rachel. "Did not I serve with thee for Rachel?" he asked of Laban (Gen: 29:25). He wanted what he had seen at the well.

God will yet bring you what He has ordained for you.

Don't settle for the appetizer! Go back to your well. Remind yourself of what God spoke to you, of all that He promised. You don't want less than that, really, do you? You may be tired now but remember that Isaiah 40:31 says that "... they that wait upon the LORD shall renew their strength; they shall mount up with wings as eagles; they shall run, and not be weary; and they shall walk, and not faint." God will give you the stamina you need to endure. He wants you to receive all that He has in mind even more than you do!

Take a deep breath, hang in there, and keep going. Commit to getting all God has for you. Remind yourself of His promises and pursue them. As you do, you might want to echo the chorus of Ricardo Clarke's song, "Not Settlin," to yourself:

> *I'm not settlin, I deserve the best. Not gonna live my life like the rest. I'm not settlin', I deserve the best. Absolutely no opinion, no contest.*

Be determined

Jacob was so in love with Rachel that he had offered to work for Laban for seven more years to earn the right to marry her. He sweated it out in the fields for eighty-four long months, but they seemed "like only a few days to him because of his love for her" (Gen. 29:20, NIV).

Jacob wanted what had been promised him so bad that he was willing to go any distance to get it. No doubt he reminded himself each morning that he was another day closer to his dream. Jacob pursued the promise (Rachel) until he got it (Gen 29:28).

How much are you willing to give in order to get? How much are you willing to give up to receive? How far are you willing to go in order to receive what God's got for you? Don't settle!

The plain fact is, as long as you can live without God's best, you will. Only when you are willing to stay hungry for more will you receive it. You must aggressively pursue God's best. That word *aggressively* means violently. You must get radical. You've got to make some decisions. Youve got to be determined!

You've got to decide, *I am not staying here! I'm moving from this position of poverty. I'm moving from this position of unhappiness. I'm moving from this position of lack. I'm moving from this position of stress. I'm moving from this position of being alone and I'm going after what God's got for me.*

And, like Jacob, you need to keep encouraged as you wait. Prayer, praise, study of God's Word, fellowship with other believers, and service can all lift our spirits and renew our strength and commitment as we wait.

God has brought you too far to quit now. Tell Him, tell yourself, and tell the enemy that you are not going to settle for less than the best of what God has for you.

Yes, there are times of struggle, when we need to press on toward what God has called us, straining for the prize like Paul did. But we are not actually struggling to make it happen, though, but rather to be in position; God can and will make it happen. Our part is to be persistent and patient in cooperating with Him.

David knew a thing or two about disappointments and delays, sidetracks and setbacks, on his way from the shepherd's hut to the king's palace. But he was able to write that though "weeping may stay for the night... rejoicing comes in the morning" (Ps. 30:5, NIV).

Keep going.

Pursue the promise.

Don't settle for the appetizer!

Chapter Three

THE PROMISE WILL MAKE YOU LAUGH

TRAVELING TO SHARE the good news of the kingdom has allowed me to meet some wonderful people in different places. I have also experienced a wide range of standards of accommodation! There have been some uncomfortable hours lying on lumpy beds—though I consider a poor night's sleep a small price to pay for the privilege of ministering to people's needs, and seeing God break through in their lives.

And then there have been occasions when I've received the truly royal treatment. Like the time I was in Dallas, Texas at a five-day conference, with accommodation provided at one of the city's finest hotels.

Walking into the lobby was almost like entering a palace. Beautiful decor, stylish furniture, attentive staff ready to cater for a visitor's every need. I wanted to sit down and savor it all for a moment. But, nice as it was, I didn't intend to stretch out on one of the sofas there for the night!

See, I was still on the ground floor. My destination was way up above, in one of the hotel's finest suites on the top floor, graciously provided by the conference hosts.

Great as the lobby was, I would have been foolish to have camped out there when there was so much more waiting for me.

That—minus the concierge service, maybe—was kind of the situation Abram found himself in when God called him to believe for more.

From the life of the man who would become the father of our faith, and for whom food offerings were an important symbol of his trust in God, are some further lessons for us as we follow in his faltering footsteps, refusing to settle for the appetizer.

Stick to your certainties

Abram had to be willing to set out without having all the answers, just as his grandson Jacob did years later, as we considered in the previous chapter. In Genesis 12, God told Abram, "Get thee out of thy country, and from thy kindred, and from thy father's house, unto a land that I will shew thee." Notice that God didn't fill in all the blanks.

He didn't say exactly where or how, but he did promise (verses 2-3), "And I will make of thee a great nation, and I will bless thee, and make thy name great; and thou shalt be a blessing: And I will bless them that bless thee, and curse them that curseth thee: and in thee shall all families of the earth be blessed."

While there was a lot Abram did not know, there was one thing he was sure of: God had spoken. He moved out in obedience. Even though his assurance that things would come to pass would waiver in the years ahead, he never seemed to doubt that he had heard God. He may not have been sure if or how God was going to do what He had said He would, but he didn't question whether it had been God speaking in the first place.

In the same way, we need to be settled in our confidence that God has spoken. There is a difference between wishful thinking and divine direction, and only the second will see us through the challenges of life that come our way. It can be helpful to spend some time reviewing what we may believe God has spoken into our lives about the future. Have there perhaps been dreams, prophetic words spoken, or other independent circumstances that confirm what we have heard?

Remember, as Paul wrote in Philippians 1:6, that "he which hath begun a good work in you will perform it until the day of Jesus Christ." When God speaks, we can take it to the bank. You can have an assurance that things are not going to remain the same.

Be willing to separate

Abram didn't have things bad in Haran when God came and told him to move. He seems to have been fairly prosperous, because when he did get ready to head out for the great unknown, Genesis recounts that he and those with him collected "all their possessions that they had acquired… and the people that they had acquired…"

Not only did Abram have stuff, he also had status. He was known in the area; presumably he had relationships he could leverage. On a practical level, it might seem to make sense that God work with all that was at hand, rather than go where he would apparently be starting from scratch.

But no, God wanted Abram to separate himself from what and who was familiar to him. How did the rest of the extended family feel when Abram said God had told him to head out for a new place? Were they offended? Did they think he was crazy? Or did some ask if they could go along too?

Sometimes we have to be willing to separate ourselves from others so that God has room to do what only He can. The reason may be clear; they are muffling our ability to hear God, or quenching the flames of our faith. But they do not have to be people who are naysayers or critics; indeed, they may be near and dear to us. Yet, like Abram, we are still called to put some distance between us and them. Don't settle for the appetizer!

When God called me into full-time ministry, he disrupted some of my closest relationships. Something shifted between us. It wasn't that there was a rift, or anything like that, but somehow I knew that I was going somewhere they had not been called, and there needed to be a degree of separation. God wanted that space to work in further down the line.

It's not just about relationships, though. God might be calling you to separate from a job, or a ministry situation. It seems good, it seems to have potential for more, but what if God's more has to come somewhere else?

This kind of separation is both a question of faith — how much will we trust Him? — and also a question of positioning — getting to where God needs us to be so He can bring about all He has promised. As Mike Murdock says, "What you are willing to walk away from determines what God will bring to you." The promise will make you laugh!

Consider the cost

Good things don't come cheap. You can sit down to a fine steak, but you are going to have to pay for it. Or you could just fill up on appetizers instead, because they are cheaper.

Some people are satisfied with driving an old clunker that they've painted up to look good, while the engine's still shot. Things look good on the outside, but there's trouble under the hood. That's a really short-term view. Surely they'd be better off buying a better car, even though it is going to cost them something.

And given that God has good things in mind for us, wouldn't it make sense to invest whatever

Good things don't come cheap.

we need to, to receive them? Why would we want to hold on to what we have, when what is being offered will be so much better? This is what Jesus had in mind when He told the parable of the pearl of great price, in Matthew 13:45-46:

> Again, the kingdom of heaven is like unto a merchant man, seeking goodly pearls: Who, when he had found one pearl of great price, went and sold all that he had, and bought it.

Abram had to be willing to say goodbye to familiarity and family, to follow God and receive all that was promised.

For some people, their motivation for settling for less isn't that they don't want to pay the price. It's that they don't think they deserve the best. If that's you, let me encourage you to think again. Remember that God the Father thought you were so valuable that He gave His only son as a ransom to bring you into relationship with Him. You are worth Jesus to Him!

God doesn't just want to save you for eternity, He wants you to experience more of His kingdom in this life. Consider the price He paid to make that available to you! Don't settle for less when He has so much more for you.

Refuse the lesser kings

Abram's journey to the fulfillment of what God had promised was long and eventful, as we all know. Having left Haran with his nephew, Lot, and then spent some time in Egypt, the two moved to the Negeb and later separated, going their own ways.

Abram suggested they split up because they were both prospering, and their herdsmen were falling out over how to care for their growing herds on limited natural resources (Gen. 13:5-7). He didn't want their business tensions to become a source of personal strife.

The move to separate areas seems to have worked. For when Abram later learned that Lot and his family and possessions had been taken captive by a group of marauding kings, he went to the rescue. There appears to have been no lingering resentment or ill-will, no thoughts of, *Serves him right*. Abram pursued the invaders, and "brought back his kinsman Lot with his possessions, and the women and the people" (Gen. 14:13-16, ESV).

Having done so, Abram was then offered a reward by the grateful king of Sodom. But Abram would have none of it. He refused to take so much as a thread or a sandal strap, "lest you should say, 'I have made Abram rich'" (Gen.14:23).

Abram did not want anyone but God to get the glory. He knew that God did not need a helping hand in bringing to pass what He had promised. He did not want a "lesser king" to be able to take any credit. Don't settle for the appetizer!

How about you? As you wait for God to bring about the fulfillment of all that He has promised you, be alert to the subtle ways in which you may be tempted to allow others to share the limelight, rather than leaving the spotlight on God. He does not need a helping hand in bringing about your destiny.

Bear in mind that these kings can look good. They may seem to be helpful, but what will be the result of accepting something from them? Will it reflect on them or on God? In Isaiah 42:8, we are reminded that God says, "I am the Lord: that is my name: and my glory will I not give to another, neither my praise to graven images."

Don't give in to fear

The enemy uses all kinds of ways to keep us from pursuing what God has in store for us. He tries to tempt us to chase after things that ultimately are not good. If that doesn't work, he will try to bury us in distractions, diversions, and delays—keeping us busy but not focused on what really matters.

But I believe one of his most common strategies is to try to scare us off. That might be why, after Abram's encounter with the king of Sodom, "the word of the Lord came unto Abram in a vision, saying, *Fear not,* Abram: I am thy shield and thy exceeding great reward" (Gen. 15:1, emphasis added).

Fear can cause you to make some terrible decisions. Fear that if you let that one person walk away, you won't find another relationship. So you stay. Fear that if you walk away from that unsatisfying job, you won't get a better one. So you stay.

Fear makes us settle for what is rather than what is to come. When the enemy tries to cause us to draw back from God, we need to press in closer. 2 Timothy 1:7 reminds us that "God hath not given us the spirit of fear; but of power, and of love, and of a sound mind." The promise will make you laugh!

Keep looking up

When God's promises seem to be a long time coming, it's only human to have doubts. The issue is, how are we going to handle them? For Abram, the secret was wrapped in God's promise to him.

After years had passed without the birth of a child to whom he could leave the wealth he had accumulated, Abram grew despondent. Looking around, he saw that his servant Eliezer would be the one to inherit everything. Abram despaired about it all to God.

"This shall not be thine heir," God answered (Gen. 15:4), "but he that shall come forth out of thine own bowels shall be thine heir." Then He took Abram outside his tent and instructed him, "Look up at the sky and count the stars — if indeed you can count them... So shall your offspring be."

God says the same thing to you today: Look up! Don't be limited by what you see around you. Don't try to work everything out practically. God may have something in mind to bring about His purposes for you that you cannot see or imagine. Remember the famous line by Dale Carnegie, "Two men looked out from prison bars, One saw the mud, the other saw stars." It's all about perspective.

Eliezer was intended to be a blessing in his master's life, but Abram let him become a limiting factor, by allowing his presence to cloud his sight. Don't choke your hope and faith by looking around at what you can see. Don't settle for what's in front of you. Don't settle for the lookalikes and the counterfeits. Set your sights higher. Look up.

Put your blinders on

Looking the right way is essential for seeing God's blessing, but social media makes it easier than ever to get distracted these days. Maybe that's why in writing to the Colossians, Paul urged them to "Set your affection on things above, not on things on the earth" (3:2). He knew that looking God's way requires effort, an act of the will; it doesn't just happen.

Race horses are magnificent creatures. Seeing them at full speed, in all their glory, is a marvelous thing. But though they are immensely powerful, they can also be very skittish, easily spooked by what's around them. That is why you will often see them fitted with blinders when they are out on the road, and sometimes even when racing.

That way they can only see straight ahead, protected from things around that may unsettle them. Perhaps you need to get yourself a pair of blinders? Are there people, pursuits, pleasures, problems on your periphery that are distracting you? Do you need to take steps to block them out of your vision so you can focus on what's straight ahead?

Abraham was surely delighted when he and Sarah welcomed their son Isaac, as centenarians. But this miracle birth wasn't the fulfillment of all that God had promised him; Abraham had been told that his descendants would be as countless as the stars.

So he must have wondered how that would ever be when God called him to sacrifice Isaac, in Genesis 22: after all, his son was the one through whom all those later generations must come. Tempting as it must have been to look about for some way around the situation, Abraham put his blinders on and looked straight ahead. He did just what God told him.

Only after he reached the point of raising his knife over Isaac at the place of sacrifice on Mount Moriah does

Abraham appear to have shifted his gaze, and then only when God told him to:

> And the angel of the Lord called unto him out of heaven, and said, Abraham, Abraham: and he said, Here am I. And he said, Lay not thine hand upon the lad, neither do thou any thing unto him: for now I know that thou fearest God, seeing thou hast not withheld thy son, thine only son from me. And Abraham lifted up his eyes, and looked, and behold behind him a ram caught in a thicket by his horns: and Abraham went and took the ram, and offered him up for a burnt offering in the stead of his son. - Genesis 22: 11-13

Sometimes, though, blinders aren't enough. If a rider is out on his horse near traffic, he might need to do something else to keep the animal settled and prevent it from rearing and getting hurt. In such situations, he will begin tapping the horse on its neck with the reins. The repetitive action is enough to keep the horse focused on what's ahead. The discomfort narrows the animal's awareness.

Sometimes, in His kindness, God also "taps" us to keep us safe and in line. Physical, relational, oppositional, and financial pressures can be His way of reducing our field of vision and awareness to what is right in front of us, protecting us from other dangers around.

Learn to be content

Imagine you're driving somewhere, and you suddenly realize that you are headed in the wrong direction. Putting the brakes on, stopping going the wrong way, is a great decision. But that's only half the solution.

Coming to a halt is the first step; now you need to go the other way.

It's the same idea when it comes to avoiding distractions and temptations that can keep us from all that God has for us. Shutting those things down is only part of the answer. We need to go another way; instead of hankering after things that won't help us, we need to learn to be content with what we have right now.

When he was offered a share in the riches he had acquired while freeing Lot from captivity, Abram declined. He chose to be satisfied with what he had.

I'm not saying that we don't still hunger for more — remember, there's a feast ahead. But while we wait for it to arrive, as we acknowledge our growing appetite, yet at the same time we are satisfied: we don't fill up on lesser things. We concentrate on what is to come, not what is available. Sarai focused on what was to hand and it led to all sorts of trouble, as we will see.

Don't settle for the appetizer!

If anyone ever knew for sure that there was more ahead, it was Paul. That glimpse of heaven he wrote about in 2 Corinthians must have left him yearning to return there. In Philippians 3:13-14 he wrote of "forgetting those things which are behind, and reaching forth unto those things which are before..."

Yet even with that hunger burning in him, he was able to say later, in Philippians 4:11, how he had "learned, in whatsoever state I am, therewith to be content." Contentment is a protection against desperation, which is a dangerous place to be. When we are desperate, we can persuade ourselves that it's okay to compromise. We convince ourselves that what used to smell off now seems like roses.

If you're tempted to do something to try to hurry along what God has promised you, remember that you wouldn't want the waiter at the restaurant to bring out the main course before it had been fully cooked: it would taste terrible. God's timing is perfect and can be trusted.

Remind yourself of Ecclesiastes 3:11, "He hath made every thing beautiful in his time..." His time, not yours!

The importance of worship

God had to remind and reassure Abram of His promises several times during the long years of waiting, but there was a pivotal moment in the journey, when Abram and Sarai were given new names in anticipation of all that was coming to them.

It arrived in Genesis 17, when God appeared to Abram and spoke of His desire to multiply him. Abram's response? Genesis 17:3 tell us that "he fell on his face."

Notice that he didn't jump up and down excitedly in anticipation of what was ahead. He fell down in front of God in the here-and-now. Abram focused on God in the present, rather than what God might have for him in the future. He was more concerned about God than what God might give him. The Giver, not the gift, as the saying goes.

We need to keep the same focus as we wait. Yes, be excited for what God has for you, but is He enough for you today? If what you are believing for never came to pass, would you still be content, because you had God all along?

Don't follow shortcuts

It's good to be open to hearing from others as we wait on God, but let me offer a word of caution. Sometimes people with the best intentions can give the worst advice! Just because they want the best for you doesn't mean they know the best way to get there. In fact, their concern for you could even cloud their judgment.

Take Abram's wife. Still childless after years of trying to conceive, she decided it was time to take things into her own hands. In Genesis 16 she tells Abram to sleep with her Egyptian slave, Hagar, and produce offspring that way.

There's a hint for us all in how the story unfolds. We're told that Abram and Sarai had been in Canaan ten years—a decade of waiting and hoping for a child. But when Abram heeded Sarai's advice, there was apparently a sudden shift in gears. Genesis 16:4 says that "he went in unto Hagar, and she conceived." There's the suggestion of immediacy in Ishmael's arrival; no waiting month after month.

Chances are, if an instant solution presents itself after a long period of waiting, what seems to be the answer could in fact be flawed. The easy things can come with hidden problems. If we act rashly, we can birth difficult circumstances.

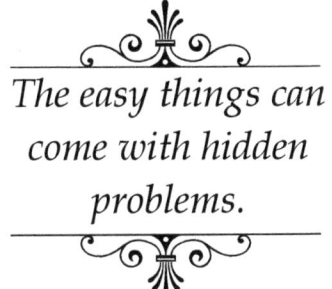

The easy things can come with hidden problems.

Spit it out

I want to receive and achieve all that God has for me, but I'm grateful that He is even more committed to doing so than I am. Because that means that our mistakes and missteps aren't final. We may blow it, but he can get us back on track.

If you over-indulge on something, the body has a way of making things right. It's not pretty, but you feel much better when what was making you feel nauseous is expelled. Sometimes, when we are sick to our stomach, we need to get rid of whatever is causing us to feel ill. Only then are we ready to really feast.

When Abraham and Sarah—as they had been renamed by God—finally welcomed their own son, Isaac, into the world, the self-made solution they had come up with became a problem.

Unhappy that now-teenage Ishmael was mocking his younger half-brother, Sarah told Abraham that his first-born and Hagar had to go. Abraham was reluctant because, after all, Ishmael was his own flesh and blood, but God told him to listen to his wife this time, hard as it seemed.

Though they were sent away into the wilderness by Abraham, Hagar and Ishmael had not been abandoned by God, of course. He guided them to water, "and God was with the lad; and he grew, and dwelt in the wilderness, and became an archer" (Gen. 21:20).

If there is a further lesson here, it is that God's grace can cover not only our mistakes, but those in turn impacted by them, as we follow his leading and commit them to his care.

Could it be that some of the bumpy things in your life are God's way of upsetting your stomach, of bringing you to a place of purging so that there is room to fill you with better things?

Be Ready to Laugh

Abraham's story doesn't just give us guidelines for receiving all that God has promised. It also offers encouragement as we find ourselves struggling with doubt, disappointment, and distractions on the way. Don't forget that while he is the father of our faith, his was not a smooth journey! The same God that persevered with Abraham is with you today.

To endure the waiting, you have to be confident of what God has promised is in store for you. But you need to be confident not just of what He has for you in the future, but of what He has already done for you, in the past, and what He is doing now.

The Promise Will Make You Laugh

He has promised that no weapon that formed against you shall stand (Isa. 54:17). He has promised that He will make a way in the wilderness and rivers in the desert (Isa. 43:19). He has promised that He will never leave you or forsake you (Heb. 13:5).

That kind of security should make you smile. Indeed, it should even make you laugh, because it is so remarkable, seemingly too good to be true.

The promise made Abraham and Sarah both laugh, too. When God appeared to Abraham when he was ninety-nine, Genesis 17 recounts, God told Abraham that Sarah would give him a son.

That made Abraham fall flat on his face, probably in a both shock and worship. And then he laughed, wondering how that could ever happen because he and his wife were so old.

When Sarah later overheard God's promise that she and Abraham would have a son, she too laughed at the apparent absurdity; after all, she was well beyond childbearing age. But sure enough, within a year Abraham and Sarah had welcomed Isaac—whose name means "laughter" in Hebrew.

Like Abraham and Sarah, your promise may seem out of reach. But remember that nothing is impossible with God. Keep pressing in to Him, and in due time your promise will make you laugh, just as Abraham and Sarah's did—but with delight, not disbelief. Don't settle for the appetizer!

Chapter Four

THE PROMISE WILL TAKE YOU HIGHER

YOU HAVE SHOWERED and washed your hair. Ladies, you've plucked and trimmed. Guys, you've shaved and smoothed. You've put on your best dress or suit, straightened things in front of the mirror one more time, and headed to the front door to wait for the car that's coming to collect you for your four-star feast. Fine dining is ahead.

No way are you going to direct your chauffeur to the drive-through to pick up some fast food. Nor are you going to settle for the cheapest and fastest items off the menu at the restaurant, when you arrive. If you'd wanted quick and convenient, you might as well have stayed home in your jammies and dialed up some home delivery!

That's kind of how it can be with stepping into the destiny God has in mind for you. You need to remind yourself that you have been invited to a banquet, that it is going to be worth the wait, and that there is some preparation and effort involved.

Don't settle for the appetizer!

Jacob and Abraham weren't the only ones who had to learn to hold out for what God had promised them. So did

Caleb: it would be forty years before he finally tasted the milk and honey God had said was on the menu. If you're at a point in your life where you are wondering whether you can hang on for the best any more, whether it might not be easier to just settle, his story also offers inspiration and insight as we anticipate what God has in store.

Remember that Caleb was one of the Israelites who followed Moses—the man who God had told would lead His people into a land "flowing with milk and honey" (Exod. 3:17)—out of slavery in Egypt. His appetizer was the manna and quail God sent for the Israelites six days a week during their trek through the wilderness.

By the time they all arrived at the edge of the Promised Land, after four decades of wandering and the same old diet, Caleb might have been forgiven for settling. The manna and quail were God's provision, after all, so why not be grateful for what he had been given and simply be content?

Because he knew there was more to come.

Recognize your sneak preview

Have you ever suddenly found yourself in your sweet spot, when everything seems to be coming together almost effortlessly? Relationships flow naturally, connections come easily opening new doors of opportunity, there is provision without striving. It's all just going so right.

I've had periods like that. People of influence gave of themselves and sowed into my life. Invitations to minister came from places I'd never have anticipated. Church membership grew, book sales went up. I was soaring!

And then, it was as though someone turned the faucet off. The flow ended. I didn't crash and burn, but I landed with a bit of a bump. I was back having to work hard again to make less progress, so it seemed.

Caleb got his taste when he was one of the twelve spies Moses sent into the Promised Land to spy out the inheritance the Israelites had been promised. The land was so bountiful that it took two of them to carry back a sample cluster of grapes (Num. 13:23) — and I suspect they may have sampled a few on the way.

But soon they would all be back to days of dust, manna, and quail.

If you have experienced something similar, let me make one thing clear. This is not God's cruelty, it's His kindness. It's not that He gives you something just to take it away, it's that He gives you a taste of something that can never be taken away from you. It's a taste of your future, stimulating your appetite for the more that's in store. Like at the movies, it's a sneak preview of a coming feature — starring you. You just have to be prepared to play your part.

Don't miss the details

If you find yourself in what feels like a "coming attractions" trailer, be sure to take in as much as you can. The glimpse of what is ahead may help sustain and motivate you as you move towards its fulfillment.

The twelve spies were given very specific instructions for their assignment. Moses didn't just ask them to wander around for a while and see how they felt about things. In Numbers 13 we see that he told them where to go and what kind of questions to ask, so that they would be able to make a good assessment.

Those kind of details would be important as year after year went by in the wilderness. Impressions fade over time, but facts remain unchanged; Caleb held onto what he knew was true. He didn't allow the passage of time to discourage him, to dismiss what he had seen and learned as wishful thinking. He still knew what he knew. Don't settle for the appetizer!

It can be helpful to make a point of journaling what God has been speaking to you, so you don't lose sight of what's important as time passes.

Look for the lessons

That sneak peek may not just be to keep you dreaming. It may be intended to get you to start planning, too. After all, the twelve spies weren't sent out to prepare an article for a travel brochure! They were commissioned for a military research effort.

Moses told his scouts not only to gauge how fruitful the land was — and bring back some evidence — but also to assess the strength of its current occupiers: "And see the land, what it is; and the people that dwelleth therein, whether they be strong or weak, few or many; And what the land is that they dwell in, whether it be good or bad; and what cities they be that they dwell in, whether in tents, or in strong holds…" (Num. 13:18-19).

Moses knew that what God intended the Israelites to possess was already in others' hands, and that a close look at what needed to be done would help when the time came. God didn't show them what was ahead to scare them off, but to prepare them and spur them on.

Are there lessons to be learned from what God has shown you about the future, about your promise? Are there things that, as you wait, you need to be getting ready for?

Prepare to go higher

Caleb never forgot what he and the others had seen on their forty-day reconnaissance trip. When Moses' successor, Joshua, prepared the Israelites finally to cross the

Jordan into the Promised Land, forty years later, Caleb reminded him of what he had been promised by Moses. "Now therefore give me this mountain, whereof the Lord spake in that day," he implored (Josh. 14:12).

Caleb knew that would mean climbing—going higher. He would not be able to stay at the level he was at. He needed to lift his sights, to look above his current situation. And he had to be willing to step up, literally, if he was going to receive all that he had been told could be his. It would be hard work, but he knew that it would be worth it.

Caleb didn't want a low-level prize, he wanted more—higher ground, a mountain. For some people, a mountain sounds more like an obstacle than a blessing, but that is not the case. It's a symbol of God's abundance, and of the heights he wants you to experience.

Don't settle for where you are: be prepared to climb!

Don't settle for where you are: be prepared to climb!

Be careful who you listen to

Caleb was one of only two of the twelve spies who later made it back into the Promised Land they had scouted out. The other was Joshua, of course. What separated them from the others? It was not that they had more information, it was what they did with what they had.

All twelve agreed that Canaan was a good place, that it did indeed flow with milk and honey, just as God had promised all those years before. But the ten added a crucial word to their report: 'Nevertheless" (Num. 13:28). In other words, *Yes, but*. They reported back that the land they had been told was theirs was already occupied… and by giants. Though Caleb tried to reassure the people they could possess the land, the other spies said, "We be not able to go up against the people; for they are stronger than we" (Num. 13:30/31).

The majority report caused the hearts of the people to "melt," Caleb would recall decades later when he finally got his chance to go back into the Promised Land (Josh. 14:8). The result: the people of God failed to enter into all that God had for them. Don't settle for the appetizer!

How important it is that we are listening to the right people about the future! The majority is not always right; sometimes it's the minority voices that are speaking the truth. If we aren't careful, we can miss out on God's more for us.

That's why it is so important we develop spiritual discernment, and learn to "test the spirits," as 1 John 4:1, admonishes.

In addition to being careful about who we listen to, we also need to be alert to the things that we say to ourselves! Because it's a silent, internal conversation, we may be unaware that we are talking to ourselves much of the time. We are affirming what we really believe deep down—about ourselves, and about God.

Look at the ten dejected spies who came back from Canaan overwhelmed by the size of the opposition they saw. "We were in our own sight as grasshoppers," they said (Num. 13:31, 33). No way could a group of grasshoppers take on a gang of giants, right? Their view of themselves determined what they believed was possible. In effect, they tied God's hands.

The key thing is to see yourself through the eyes of faith. Remind yourself that "I can do all things through Christ which strengtheneth me" (Phil. 4:13). This will help you develop the mindset that says, *I must win, I must not quit. So I will not quit, and I will win. Go for the main course!*

Are there ways in which you may be inadvertently undermining what God wants to do in your life and for you, because of how you see yourself and Him? Ask God to show you how you really see things, and for Him to correct any distorted vision so that you see more accurately!

Learn to be faithful

You may not be waiting on your promise because of what someone else failed to do, as Caleb had to, but there are still things to learn from how he came through those long years. We don't know much about the details of what he did during all that time, but we can make an assumption about his manner—that he remained convinced of God's good promises.

While the other Israelites grumbled as they wandered around in the wilderness, Caleb "wholly followed the LORD God of Israel" (Josh. 14:14). He continued to walk in God's ways, even as he waited. In the same way, while you wait for what God has promised you, you can show your love for Him by living according to His Word.

Sometimes people get hung up about what God has for them or wants them to do in the future and overlook the present. As I have said previously, while you seek His direction for tomorrow, He has given plenty for you to do today: "He hath shewed thee, O man, what is good; and what doth the LORD require of thee, but to do justly, and to love mercy, and to walk humbly with thy God?" (Micah 6:8).

You can be busy doing those three things in your everyday life without a sense of what God wants you to do as a vocation and where He may want you to live. Like Caleb, you can be wholehearted for God today even as you look forward to tomorrow. Obedience doesn't need to wait for further revelation.

It's also worth remembering that people are watching you while you wait. They want to see what God means to you in the waiting, not just in the good and full times. Anyone can give glory to God when things are going well, but what about before the blessing comes? Do people see you still trusting and honoring God, believing He has good things in store even though you don't know how He is going to work it all out? We must remain faithful, believing what God shows us, without trying to figure out how He's going to get it done.

Don't settle for the appetizer!

Giants are a good sign!

Opposition can be good. If there are people and things in your way, it's likely an indication that you are on the right track. There were giants occupying the land that Caleb had been promised for a reason—it was good! It was flowing with the milk and honey he had been promised way back when, with the other Israelites held in bondage in Egypt, he heard God's promise of deliverance and abundance, through Moses (Exod. 3:17).

If the Promised Land had been bleak and barren, there wouldn't have been people determined to keep possession of it; they'd have gone looking for a better place to live themselves. So don't be too discouraged if you find yourself facing a challenge to your destiny.

The "sitting tenants" that Caleb had to dislodge to claim his inheritance were no run-of-the-mill enemy. They were the Anakim, a giant, warlike people. It was they who had been at the root of the ten spies' despair forty years earlier when they returned from their reconnaissance to warn of people "stronger than we... the giants, the sons of Anak, which come of the giants: and we were in our own sight as grasshoppers, and so we were in their sight" (Num. 13:31, 33).

I have faced my own giants. They didn't stand head and shoulders above me physically, but they had stature and influence. For some reason, they seemed to want to do everything they could to hinder my success, to block me. It wasn't outright attack, so much as indirect.

Whether it is on the job, in the church or your own business, once you are pursuing the greater, there is going to be a giant in your way. They are there to discourage you, to make you feel like you can't get by them.

Before you let your shoulders sag in defeat, remember that what God has promised you is near — it's just over there. You simply have to go and take possession. That relationship breakthrough you have been promised? That career advancement? That greater level in ministry? The peace? It's close at hand. You've had a taste. Don't settle for the appetizer!

The Israelites were just a few hours away from milk and honey when they shrank back. Don't give up now, because you are almost there. Don't let anyone stand in your way. No matter how big they may seem.

Funny as it might sound at first, it's important to remember that giants come in all shapes and sizes. They could be actual people, like those who wanted to thwart my growing ministry. They might be financial or practical challenges that seem insurmountable. What they have in common is their aim, to make us shrink back in one way or another.

Just like the Israelites did when they turned away from the Promised Land and headed back into the wilderness. And just like they did years later when facing Goliath.

Get ready to fight

Some Christians misunderstand God's goodness and grace. They think that because He is so loving, He will make everything easy for us. But the reality is, because He is loving He doesn't always make things easy for us.

Pretty much anything worth having in this world will cost you something. Money. Time. Effort. The same thing is true spiritually. God had a land flowing with milk and honey in mind for His chosen people, but they would have to fight for it. It wouldn't just come to them on a silver platter.

Why was that? In part because, in the words of that old saying, *easy come, easy go*. If you haven't put any effort into getting something, chances are you won't try too hard to hold onto it. But we live in a world where an enemy is always looking to take away what God has given us. "The thief cometh not, but for to steal, and to kill, and to destroy," Jesus warned (John 10:10).

The great thing is, though, that we do not fight alone, of course. God is on our side. Ultimately it is His fight and His victory, but He wants us to be a part of it. He uses the giants to pull the best out of us, and they do. It's the oppositions, that God uses to build your resistance and make you a fighter, that will never cut and run at the first sign of difficulty.

When God opens doors for us, there will always be an enemy that will try to push them shut, that will try to get us to settle for what's outside the door, and never discover what's inside. What are you going to do when you see one closing? Just accept it and meekly go looking somewhere else?

Maybe you need to stay there and keep knocking. Demand that it open up because what's yours is just behind it! Whomever it may be that is standing at the door, pushing it closed, because they don't want you to get what's yours. Trying to block you so you become discouraged and settle, will soon realize–that you were built for battle. Don't settle for the appetizer, but rather, pursue the main course – all that God has for you.

I'm reminded of a New Testament time when four men found a door blocked. They were trying to take their friend to Jesus for healing, but the place was so full they could not get in. They were not going to be deterred, though. So, Mark 2 recounts, they went up on the roof and made a hole in it so they could lower their friend down in front of Jesus.

Maybe if your door is blocked you need to think about finding another way in! How about "raising the roof" — not physically, but in prayer, praise and worship, declaring God's goodness over and above all obstacles?

Are we going to be like the ten spies, who saw only the challenge, the closed door, or like Caleb and Joshua? They agreed that there were giants in the land — but they reminded the people that God had said He would be with them, and with God on their side they were bound to be victorious.

Facing down your giant

David the shepherd boy is the most famous giant-killer of all time, of course. The way he ran out to confront Goliath armed with only a slingshot and five smooth stones should inspire us to follow in his footsteps. Like him, we can trust that the God who has protected us thus far — David recounted how, with God's help, he had taken down both lions and bears (1 Sam. 17:36) — will be with us.

I wonder whether if, in addition to looking back on God's hand on his own life, David also thought back to and drew courage from the example of Caleb. When Caleb and Joshua reported back to Moses and the people about what they had seen in Canaan, they didn't downplay the realities. They did not deny that the Anakites were bigger than the Israelites — they just went on to remind everyone that the Anakites were still much smaller than God. They didn't look at the challenge from their level, having to crane their necks up to who was towering above them. They looked at it from God's level.

"Neither fear ye the people of the land; for they are bread for us," the pair urged the people, "their defence is departed from them, and the Lord is with us: fear them not" (Num. 14:9).

You can't get to where you want to be by keeping out of the way of people who are standing in your way. At some point, you are going to have to get in that giant's face, like David did in the valley of Elah, or like Caleb did in the hill country of Canaan. I don't mean that you need to get ugly, but you will have to stand up and show that you are not intimidated by their size and their swagger. Don't settle for the appetizer!

Don't let the giants convince you into settling for less than God's best for your life. Don't settle for where you are, but push forward to where you're going. The main course!

Don't settle. Share the confidence of Caleb: "If so be the LORD will be with me, then I shall be able to drive them out, as the LORD said" (Josh. 14:12). Echo the words of David to Goliath: "Thou comest to me with a sword, and with a spear, and with a shield: but I come to thee in the name of the LORD of hosts, the God of the armies of Israel, whom thou hast defied" (1 Sam. 17:45).

Don't let the giants convince you into settling

The enemy wants to get us to break down before we reach our breakthrough. Stand firm. Hold fast to Paul's encouragement in Galatians 6:9: "And let us not be weary in well doing: for in due season we shall reap, if we faint not."

It is never too late

There is a final piece of encouragement from Caleb's example, for those who may be feeling that, for whatever reason, they've missed their chance for more. You held on to a promise for a long time, but now it just seems somehow that it's too late. You're still single well past your prime, retirement is getting closer and that promotion didn't come through. The children are almost grown and that bigger house never materialized.

Why keep hoping, believing, and pressing for something that maybe doesn't seem worth all the effort any more. Why not just settle for the appetizer after all?

Because God's ways are not our ways, and His timing is not our timing. You might have only a couple of years in that new position before it's time to retire, not the long tenure you'd anticipated. But who knows what impact you might have in even a short season? After all, as 2 Peter 3:8-9 reminds us, "one day is with the Lord as a thousand years, and a thousand years as one day. The Lord is not slack concerning his promise..."

When Joshua brought the Israelites to the edge of the Promised Land after their forty-year detour, Caleb might have been forgiven for thinking, *I'll just leave it to the younger ones.* But he was determined to see the fulfillment of what he had been promised, even at an advanced age.

He told Joshua, "As yet I am as strong this day as I was in the day that Moses sent me: as my strength was then, even so is my strength now, for war, both to go out, and to come in. Now therefore give me this mountain, whereof the LORD spake in that day; for thou heardest in that day how the Anakims were there, and that the cities were great and fenced: if so be the LORD will be with me, then I shall be able to drive them out, as the LORD said" (Josh. 14:11-12). Don't settle for the appetizer!

Where did Caleb find that drive and fire from? Perhaps in part from the example of Moses, who himself had refused to allow time and age to disqualify him. As a young man, his concern for his fellow Jews had been poorly managed; after killing the Egyptian overseer who had been abusing a Jewish slave, Moses was forced to flee the country. He languished in Midian for forty years — the same amount of time Caleb wandered in the desert—before God sent him back as his countrymen's deliverer.

Yes, Moses was initially reluctant to step into his role, but in doing so he became a channel of God's deliverance to others. In the same way, what God yet has for you may be a channel of blessing to others. Don't miss out on it by discounting yourself wrongly. It's never too late with or for God.

Not that it will come easy just because you're older. Caleb still had to go and fight for what was his. But he didn't want to miss out on his mountain, and he knew that God was with him.

Given the fear that the Anakites had struck in the hearts of the spies and the rest of the people forty years earlier, their fearsomeness the reason the Israelites did not go over in to the Promised Land, you might expect that when the battle finally came it would be a big event.

But that does not seem to have been the case. There's no account of a major clash. Joshua 15:14 simply notes that "Caleb drove out the three Anakites—Sheshai, Ahiman and Talmai, the sons of Anak." It's a simple statement of fact, as though it were no big deal.

If you're weary, and the prospects of fighting for what's yours seem overwhelming, take encouragement from God's promises. The prophet Isaiah recognizes that even young men get tired, sometimes. "But those who hope in the Lord will renew their strength," he goes on (Isa. 40:30-31, NIV). "They will soar on wings like eagles; they will run and not grow weary, they will walk and not be faint."

I'm not an old man yet, but I have been beat down and tired. There were occasions when I felt like giving up, when the giants seemed too big. There were surprise attacks from people I trusted and loved. Friends walked away just when I needed them most. There was financial hardship.

But I chose to press in to God, to look to Him, to believe Him. I stood up to my giants, and they gave way. God allowed those challenges to forge in me a tenacious spirit, that keeps me pressing towards the main course. Give me my mountain!

If God has spoke something over your life, as he did with Caleb, don't miss out on your mountain.

Don't settle for the appetizer!

Chapter Five

AFTERWORD

Remembering the Main Thing

HAVING STARTED THIS book with the story of a meal, it's appropriate to end with one also. As I mentioned at the beginning, I enjoy sharing good food in good company. Indeed, it can be a foretaste of heaven: think how Revelation 19:9 says "blessed are they which are called unto the marriage supper of the Lamb." One day we will dine with Jesus in the New Jerusalem. What a celebration that is going to be!

Being able to savor nourishment with special people is a blessing. But that doesn't have to mean a fancy restaurant and a menu with things on it that you can't pronounce. In fact, much as I appreciate a great dining-out experience, some of the most meaningful moments I have experienced, when I have been closest to heaven, have been in simpler settings, with the most basic of elements.

I'm referring to communion, of course, when we recall The Last Supper. A small portion of bread and a sip of grape juice. They may not fill me physically, but they do fill me spiritually, reminding me that even as I look forward to and hope for all that God has for me in the future, choosing not to settle for the appetizer, at the same time, I already have all I could ever want.

Because He is a good Father, I believe that God has blessings He wants to pour into our lives—in our families and homes, in our careers and our work, in our relationships and our ministry for Him. But while we look forward to all of that, we mustn't lose sight of the fact that we already have the greatest gift we could ever receive: salvation.

Once we were dead in our sins and separated from God. We were without hope in this world. But because of His great love, revealed in the death and resurrection of Jesus Christ, we have been brought out of darkness and into His wonderful light. We are now the "children of God" (1 John 3:1). It just cannot get any better than that!

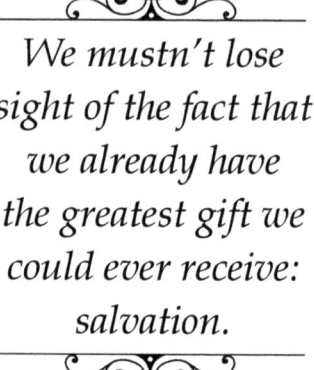

We mustn't lose sight of the fact that we already have the greatest gift we could ever receive: salvation.

Early in His ministry, Jesus appointed a group of his followers to go out and preach the good news of the kingdom and heal the sick. When they came back, they were excited at how God had used them. In Luke 10:17, we read, "And the seventy returned again with joy, saying, Lord, even the devils are subject unto us through thy name."

Jesus' response? "... in this rejoice not, that the spirits are subject unto you; but rather rejoice, because your names are written in heaven" (verse 20). In other words, *That's great. But don't forget the main thing.*

After all—and this is a sobering reminder to us all—what we consider to be a sign of God's favor may not be. Remember that some of those expecting a seat at the heavenly banquet are going to be surprised when they learn that they are not on the guest list.

Afterword

Jesus warned in Matthew 7:22-23, "Many will say to me in that day, Lord, Lord, have we not prophesied in thy name? and in thy name have cast out devils? and in thy name done many wonderful works? And then will I profess unto them, I never knew you: depart from me, ye that work iniquity."

Let me close by encouraging you to believe that God has good things in store for you. Be patient, be expectant, be faithful, be persistent, be confident.

Remember those we have followed in these pages. Be encouraged by the way Jacob endured, finally taking Rachel as his own. Be inspired by how Abram refused to let setbacks keep him from seeing God's promise realized. Be motivated by Caleb's example, not letting age and the passage of time disqualify him from taking possession of his mountain.

Likewise, if you refuse to settle, then in due season you will receive what God has for you. But just remember that, when it comes to what we look forward to in eternity, any blessings we might get to enjoy in this life are, ultimately, only appetizers.

Compared to sitting at the heavenly banquet table with Jesus, dining with Him in the New Jerusalem, anything here can only be a taste. So, above all, focus on God more than the good things He has promised. Be clear that having your name on the eternal seating plan is ultimately more important than what's on this life's menu. Don't settle for the appetizer!

ABOUT THE AUTHOR

APOSTLE DR. RENO I. Johnson is a man guided by the Holy Spirit; he is an ambassador of Christ, he is a Warrior in the faith, an excellent Teacher of God's Word and a Dynamic, Radical Preacher. In addition, he is an author, who has written many books that have broaden the scope of individuals globally and they have helped to usher lost souls into the Kingdom of God. In every dispensation throughout biblical history God has chosen men after his own heart. There was Moses, Joshua, David, Elijah, Paul, and now in our generation Apostle Johnson. He is the son of Patricia and Ivan Johnson. He is married to Shandaly Johnson and has one son and two daughters.

Apostle Johnson was ordained as a Minister at The Voice of Deliverance Disciple Center Ministries, Nassau Bahamas where he served for over thirteen years. By divine appointment today, the call and power of God is being demonstrated in the life of Apostle Johnson in such an awesome way. His unconditional love for people and passion for God's Word has been a transportation that has taken him throughout The World at large preaching the Good News of the Gospel of Jesus Christ.

Most notably, he is the president and Chief Executive Officer (CEO) of Reno I. Johnson Ministries International. He was consecrated to the Office of an Apostle on Sunday, December 5, 2010. He is also the founding pastor of Total Life Church, Altamonte Springs, Florida and Divine Encounter Ministries International in Nassau, The Bahamas.

Equally important, he has obtained an Associate Degree from New England Institute of Technology- West Palm Beach, Florida. However, upon receiving the call to ministry Apostle Johnson pursued several Biblical Degrees including a Diploma in Biblical Studies from Liberty University (Lynchburg, Virginia), an Associate Degree in Biblical Studies, and also an Honorary Doctorate Degree in Theology from Bethel Christian University, At present, he is pursuing higher academia in Theology.

Apostle Johnson is a highly sought after anointed messenger of God, whose passion is to win souls for Christ, and advance the Kingdom of God. **Touching people, Transforming lives**

CONTACT THE AUTHOR

You can email the author at
rijmintl@gmail.com or renoijohnson@gmail.com

Please visit the author's website for current phone numbers and address.
www.renoijohnson.org or www.arjm.org

To order any of Apostle Dr. Reno I. Johnson's Ministry Resources
Please visit our website, write or call us Today!

For Speaking Engagements please call, email or visit our website Today.

Connect with us on social media

Don't forget to visit our Website!

OTHER BOOKS BY THE AUTHOR:

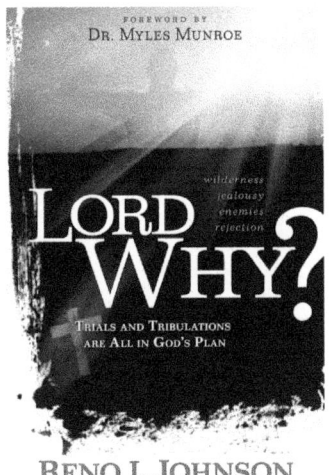
Lord Why?

Born To Reign

In Your Face

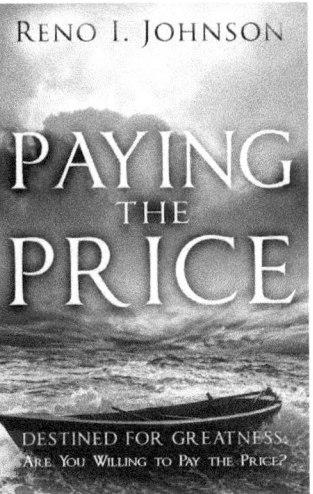
Paying The Price

www.ingramcontent.com/pod-product-compliance
Ingram Content Group UK Ltd.
Pitfield, Milton Keynes, MK11 3LW, UK
UKHW021304180426
11947UKWH00015B/1004